MUSICAL INSTRUMENTS

Djembes

Kimberly M. Hutmacher
and John Willis

AV2
www.av2books.com

AV2

Step 1
Go to **www.av2books.com**

Step 2
Enter this unique code
AHJCUB5WO

Step 3
Explore your interactive eBook!

AV2 is optimized for use on any device

Your interactive eBook comes with...

Read

Audio
Listen to the entire book read aloud

Videos
Watch informative video clips

Weblinks
Gain additional information for research

Try This!
Complete activities and hands-on experiments

Key Words
Study vocabulary, and complete a matching word activity

Quizzes
Test your knowledge

Slideshows
View images and captions

View new titles and product videos at www.av2books.com

Djembes Contents

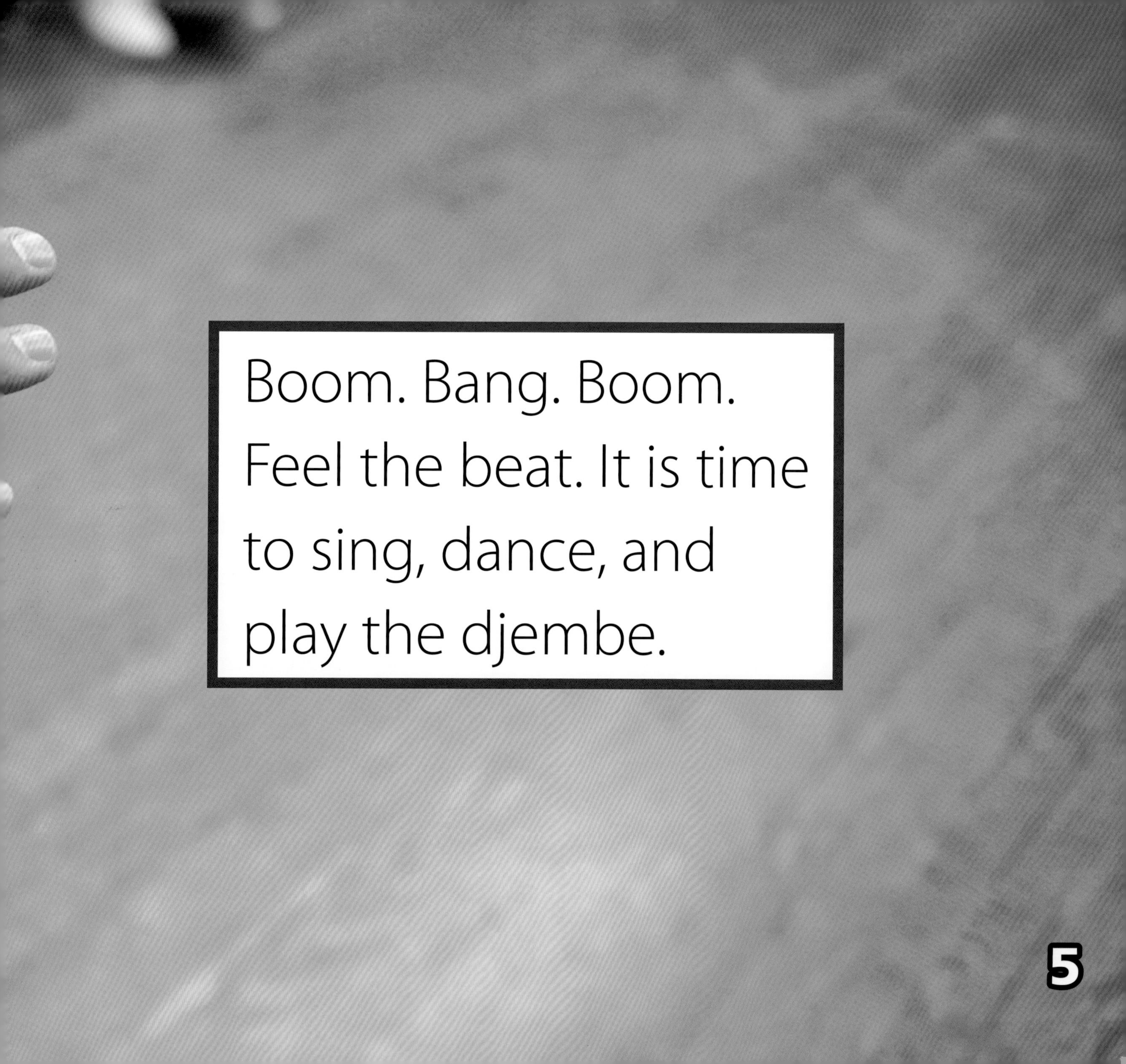

Boom. Bang. Boom. Feel the beat. It is time to sing, dance, and play the djembe.

The djembe is a drum. It is carved from a tree trunk. A djembe has a large top. The top is covered in goat skin.

A djembe is made from just one tree trunk.

Djembes are loud musical instruments. People play the djembe by hitting it with both hands.

Djembe drummers sit or stand. The djembe can be held between the drummer's legs.

A djembe is usually 23 to 25 inches high. (58 to 64 centimeters)

The djembe makes three main sounds. A low sound is called a bass. A medium sound is called a tone. A high sound is a slap.

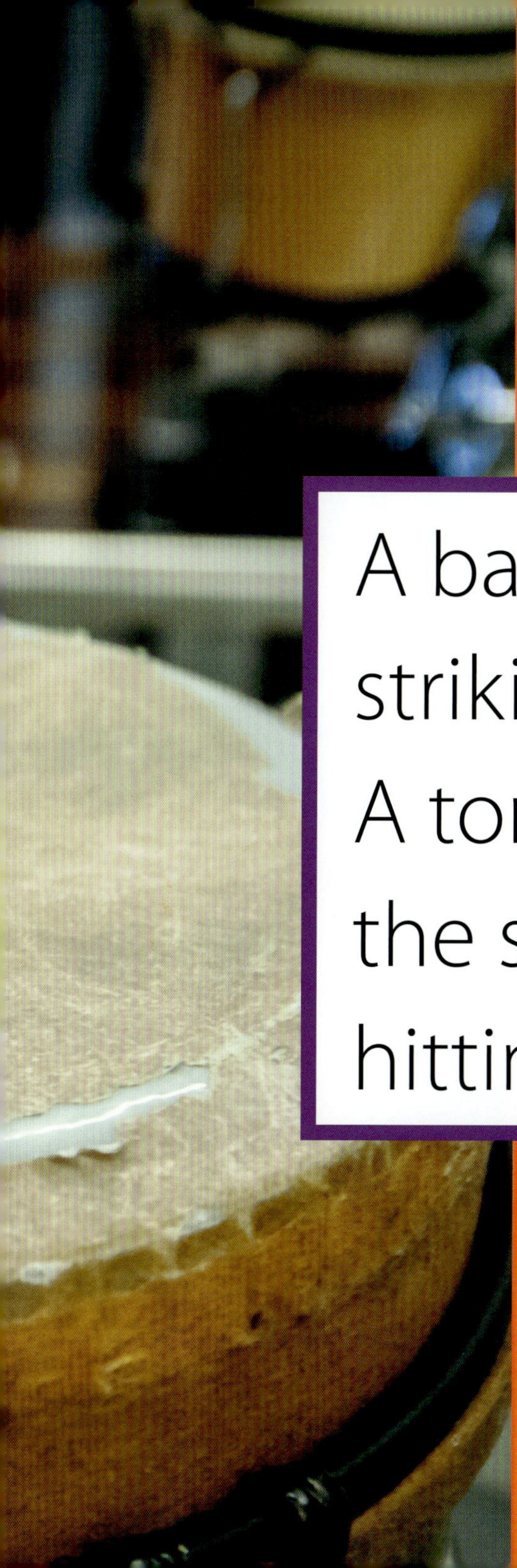

A bass sound is made by striking the drum's center. A tone is made by hitting the sides. A slap is made by hitting the djembe's edge.

The djembe was invented in Western Africa. It was made by people called the Mandinka.

The djembe is more than 800 years old.

Djembe drummers often sing and dance. The djembe is enjoyed at festivals. It is also played at birthdays and funerals.

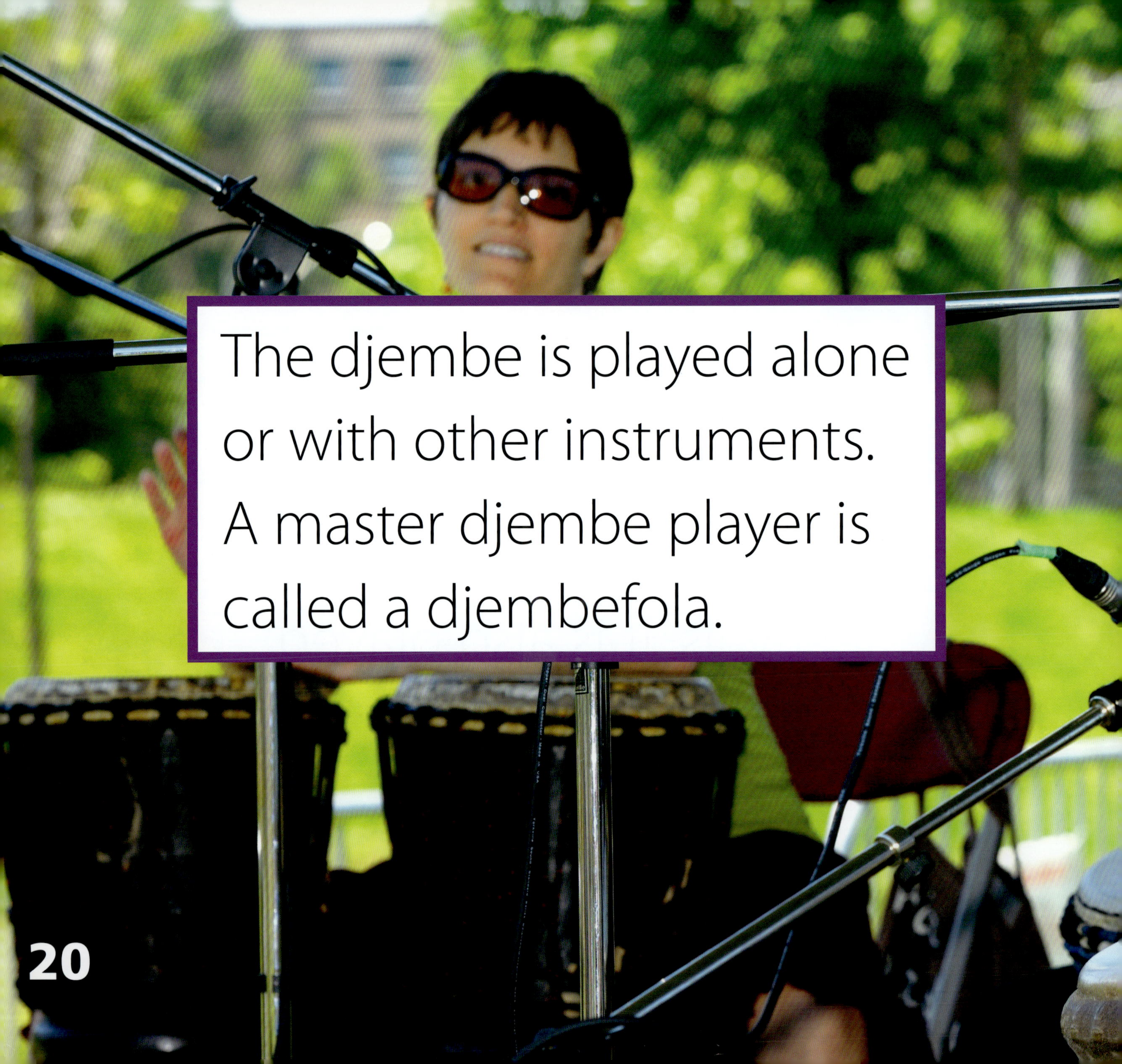

The djembe is played alone or with other instruments. A master djembe player is called a djembefola.

See what you have learned about djembes.

Which of these pictures does not show a djembe?

KEY WORDS

Research has shown that as much as 65 percent of all written material published in English is made up of 300 words. These 300 words cannot be taught using pictures or learned by sounding them out. They must be recognized by sight. This book contains 40 common sight words to help young readers improve their reading fluency and comprehension. This book also teaches young readers several important content words, such as proper nouns. These words are paired with pictures to aid in learning and improve understanding.

Page	Sight Words First Appearance
5	and, is, it, play, the, time, to
6	a, from, has, in, just, large, made, one, tree
9	are, both, by, hands, people, with
10	be, between, can, high, or
12	makes, sounds, three
15	sides
16	more, old, than, was, years
19	also, at, often
20	other

Page	Content Words First Appearance
5	beat, djembe
6	drum, goat skin, trunk
9	musical instruments
10	drummers, inches, legs
12	bass, slap, tone
15	center, edge
16	Mandinka, Western Africa
19	birthdays, festivals, funerals
20	djembefola, player

Published by AV2
350 5th Avenue, 59th Floor New York, NY 10118
Website: www.av2books.com

Library of Congress Cataloging-in-Publication Data

Names: Hutmacher, Kimberly, author.
Title: Djembes / Kimberly M. Hutmacher and John Willis.
Description: New York, NY : AV2, 2020. | Series: Musical instruments |
Audience: Ages 6-9 | Audience: Grades K-1 |
Identifiers: LCCN 2019041043 (print) | LCCN 2019041044 (ebook) | ISBN 9781791116200 (library binding) |
ISBN 9781791116217 (paperback) | ISBN 9781791116224 | ISBN 9781791116231
Subjects: LCSH: Djembe--Juvenile literature. | CYAC: Djembe.

Classification: LCC ML1038.D54 H88 2020 (print) | LCC ML1038.D54 (ebook) | DDC 786.9/319--dc23
LC record available at https://lccn.loc.gov/2019041043
LC ebook record available at https://lccn.loc.gov/2019041044

Printed in Guangzhou, China
1 2 3 4 5 6 7 8 9 0 24 23 22 21 20

022020
100919

Project Coordinator: John Willis Designer: Ana María Vidal

The publisher acknowledges Alamy, Getty Images, iStock, and Shutterstock as the primary image suppliers for this title.